Beginner Biography

Jackie Robinson

Baseball's Second-Base Hero

by Jennifer Marino Walters
illustrated by Scott R. Brooks

LOOK! BOOKS™

Red Chair Press Egremont, Massachusetts

Look! Books are produced and published by Red Chair Press:
Red Chair Press LLC PO Box 333 South Egremont, MA 01258-0333
www.redchairpress.com

FREE lesson guide at www.redchairpress.com/free-activities

Publisher's Cataloging-In-Publication Data
(Provided by Cassidy Cataloguing Services, Inc.)
Names: Marino Walters, Jennifer, author. | Brooks, Scott R., illustrator.
Title: Jackie Robinson : baseball's second-base hero / by Jennifer Marino Walters ; illustrated by Scott R. Brooks.

Other titles: Look! books (Red Chair Press). Beginner biography

Description: Egremont, Massachusetts : Red Chair Press, [2024] | Includes index. | Interest age level: 006-009. | Summary: Jackie Robinson was the first African American to play baseball in the modern major leagues. Today there are many great Black players in the MLB, but in 1947 it was very big news when Jackie stepped up to the plate. He opened doors for young Black athletes even today.--Publisher.

Identifiers: ISBN: 9781643712512 (library hardcover) | 9781643712574 (softcover) | 9781643712635 (ebook) | LCCN: 2022943800

Subjects: LCSH: Robinson, Jackie, 1919-1972--Juvenile literature. | African American baseball players--Biography--Juvenile literature. | Racism in sports--United States--History--20th century--Juvenile literature. | CYAC: Robinson, Jackie, 1919-1972. | African American baseball players--Biography. | Racism in sports--United States--History--20th century. | LCGFT: Biographies. | BISAC: JUVENILE NONFICTION / Social Topics / Prejudice & Racism. | JUVENILE NONFICTION / People & Places / United States / African American & Black. | JUVENILE NONFICTION / Sports & Recreation / Baseball & Softball.

Classification: LCC: GV865.R6 M37 2024 | DDC: 796.357092--dc23

Photo credits: 12 Library of Congress; 18, 20, 22 Courtesy of UCLA

Printed in the United States of America

0324 1P CGF24

Table of Contents

A Tough Childhood 4
Sports Star. 6
Negro Leagues 8
Making History 10
Facing Hate 14
Fighting for Rights 16
A Lasting Legacy. 18
Big Dates in Jackie's Life 22
Words to Know. 23
Learn More at the Library 23
Index. 24

A Tough Childhood

Jackie Robinson had a very hard childhood. His father left the family a year after Jackie was born in Cairo, Georgia on January 31, 1919. Jackie moved with his mother and four older siblings to Pasadena, California. Jackie was not even 2-years old when the family moved.

The family was very poor. There weren't many Black people in Pasadena. Jackie and his friends were often left out of sports and other activities.

Sports Star

That changed when Jackie went to high school in 1935. There, he played many sports. He earned **varsity letters** in baseball, basketball, football, and track.

Jackie later earned varsity letters in the same four sports at the University of California, Los Angeles. He was the first UCLA student to ever do so.

Good to Know

Jackie's older brother Mack won a silver medal in the 200-meter dash at the 1936 Olympic Games in Berlin, Germany.

Negro Leagues

After college, Jackie played semi-professional football for two years in Hawaii and California. He was **drafted** into the U.S. Army during World War II. He served from 1942–1944, but never went to war.

Soon, Jackie returned to baseball. In early 1945, he joined the **Negro** Leagues, a professional baseball league for African American players. At the time, Blacks were not allowed to play Major League Baseball (MLB).

Making History

But a man named Branch Rickey wanted to change that. He was the general manager of the Brooklyn Dodgers. His goal was to **integrate** Major League Baseball. He thought it would be good for the game and for the nation.

Good to Know

Moses Fleetwood Walker was the first Black player to ever play Major League Baseball. He played 42 games with the Toledo Blue Stockings in 1884. After that, MLB owners agreed to keep Black players out of the league.

Branch was looking for a Black player to join the Dodgers. This person had to be more than just a good baseball player. He also had to be very strong and brave. That's because many white people were against allowing Black players into the major leagues.

After Branch met Jackie, he knew he had found the right person. In 1946, Jackie joined the Dodgers' minor-league team, the Montreal Royals. He played very well and quickly earned a spot with the Dodgers.

Good to Know

Jackie hit a home run at his first Montreal game on April 14, 1946.

On April 15, 1947, Jackie stepped onto Ebbets Field in Brooklyn for the first time as a Dodger. He became the first Black player in the 20th century to play for an MLB team.

Facing Hate

It wasn't easy for Jackie. Some of his new teammates did not accept him. Many fans and players screamed racist insults at him during games. He received hate mail and death threats. But he didn't let that stop him.

In his first year with the Dodgers, Jackie won MLB's first Rookie of the Year award. In 1949, he earned the National League Most Valuable Player award.

Fighting for Rights

Every season from 1949–1954, Jackie was an All Star. In 1955, he and the Dodgers beat the New York Yankees to win the World Series championship.

Jackie retired from baseball on January 5, 1957. He became active in **civil rights** groups. He spoke out against racial discrimination, joined marches, and called for integration in all sports.

Good to Know

In his 10-season career with the Dodgers, Jackie had 1,518 hits, 137 home runs, and 197 stolen bases.

A Lasting Legacy

In 1972, Jackie died of a heart attack at age 53. His wife, Rachel, continued his **legacy** by starting the Jackie Robinson Foundation. It provides money for college and other help to students of all backgrounds.

A statue honoring Jackie is on the campus of UCLA.

In 1997, Jackie's jersey number, 42, was retired by every major-league team. That means no other MLB player can ever have that number. It is a way to remind us all that there will never again be anyone as talented and brave as #42 Jackie Robinson.

But each year, every MLB player wears 42 on April 15. That day is known as Jackie Robinson Day.

Jackie will always be remembered for breaking Major League Baseball's color **barrier**. He opened the door for Black players in baseball and other professional sports.

JACKIE ROBINSON DAY
42
APRIL 15
JACKIE ROBINSON
1919- 1972

Timeline: Big Dates in Jackie's Life

1919: Jackie is born in Cairo, Georgia.

1939: Jackie enrolls at UCLA where he stars in football and track

1942-1944: Jackie serves in the U.S. Army.

1945: He joins the Kansas City Monarchs, a Negro League baseball team.

1946: Jackie marries wife Rachel and joins the Montreal Royals, the Brooklyn Dodgers' minor-league team.

1947: Jackie plays his first game with the Brooklyn Dodgers, becoming the first Black person to play Major League Baseball in the 20th century.

Track was one of 4 sports Jackie starred in at UCLA.

1955: He helps the Dodgers win the World Series against the New York Yankees.

1957: Jackie retires from baseball.

1962: He becomes the first Black player inducted into the National Baseball Hall of Fame.

1972: Jackie dies at age 52.

1997: Jackie's jersey number, 42, is retired by every MLB team.

Words to Know

barrier: something that stops another thing

civil rights: rights that every person should have regardless of race, gender, or religion

discrimination: unfairly treating a group of people differently from another group

drafted: ordered to join the military

integrate: to end a rule that keeps people of different races apart

legacy: something that comes from someone in the past

Negro: a word used before the 1970s to refer to dark-skinned people

varsity letters: awards for excellence in a sport

Learn More at the Library

(Check out these books to read with others.)

Herman, Gail. *Who Was Jackie Robinson?* Penguin Workshop, 2010.

Robinson, Sharon. *Jackie Robinson: American Hero.* Scholastic, 2013.

Thorpe, Alexandra. *The Story of Jackie Robinson.* Rockridge Press, 2021.

Index

Brooklyn Dodgers 10–13
Georgia 4
Major League Baseball 9–10, 19, 20
Montreal Royals 12
Negro Leagues 9
Pasadena, CA 4–5
Rickey, Branch. 10–12
UCLA. 6
U.S. Army 8
World Series 16

About the Author

Jennifer Marino Walters and her husband live with their twin boys and daughter in the Washington D.C. area. The family spends many days at the ballpark watching the Nationals or cheering on the kids and their friends in Little League games. Baseball is loved by the Walters family.